Also by Nick Butterworth and Mick Inkpen:

The House on the Rock, The Lost Sheep,
The Two Sons, The Precious Pearl,
The Magpie's Story, The Mouse's Story,
The Fox's Story, The Cat's Story.

DB WS

Marshall Morgan and Scott
Marshall Pickering
34 — 42 Cleveland Street, London, W1P 5FB, U.K.

Copyright © 1989 Nick Butterworth & Mick Inkpen
First published in 1989 by Marshall Morgan and Scott Publications Ltd
Part of the Marshall Pickering Holdings Group

A subsidiary of the Zondervan Corporation

First published in the USA by
Zondervan Publishing House, 1415 Lake Drive, S.E.,
Grand Rapids, Michigan 49506

British Library CIP Data
Butterworth, Nick
   The good Samaritan
   I. Bible. N.T. Parables: Good Samaritan
   I. Title   II. Inkpen, Mick   III. Series
   226'.8

   cat. # 19104
   ISBN 0–310–55940–5

Printed and bound in Italy

The Good Stranger

Nick Butterworth and Mick Inkpen

Zondervan Publishing House
Grand Rapids, Michigan

Here is a man. He is going on a long journey.

He packs some sandwiches and some water. Then he climbs onto his donkey.

"Giddyup!"

Soon he has left the town behind him.

The sun is hot and the long climb up into the hills makes his donkey puff.

The path winds between high rocks. It is a dark place, full of shadows.

"I don't like it here," says the man. He has a funny feeling that someone is watching him.

Suddenly there is a shout!
Robbers! Three of them!

They steal his donkey and
all his belongings. And they
whack him on the head
with his own stick!

Poor man. He is left lying on the path. His head is bleeding and he cannot move his legs.

He lies here for a long time. Then, finally, he falls asleep.

After a while, someone comes
along the path. He is wearing
fine clothes. A bishop.

He stops, then hurries past,
pretending not to see. Perhaps
he is late for important business.

Perhaps he is afraid.

The man wakes up and starts
to call for help.

Ah! Here comes someone.
A man in a robe. A judge.

"Help! Help!"

But the judge pretends not
to hear and he hurries past.
Just like the bishop.

The sun rises high in the sky. The man is hot. His throat is dry. But here come more footsteps! Who is it?

Oh no! It is a stranger from a foreign country. He has no friends here. Why should he stop to help?

But the stranger does stop.
He speaks kindly to the man in
foreign words, and helps him
to drink some water.

He washes his wounds and
carefully puts a bandage round
his head.

The stranger helps the man
up onto his donkey. He puts his
arm around him to keep him from
falling off, and gently leads
him down the path.

At the next town the stranger
finds an inn. He puts the man
to bed and pays the innkeeper.

"Look after him," he says,
"until I get back."

Jesus says, "Which one was like a good neighbor?
The bishop, the judge or the stranger?"